An Entrepreneurial Therapy Guide to Overcome Self-Doubt

Guided Journal

Copyright

Printed in the United States of America
Book Written by Katie Onitiri-Hageman, LMFT
Book design by Shruti Rajput

First Printing, 2022

ISBN 978-0-578-36247-2

Table of Contents

This Journal belongs to:

Introduction

A study completed by the National Institute of Mental Health indicates that 49% of entrepreneurs deal with mental health issues directly. According to Michael Freeman's findings, entrepreneurs are:

- Twice as likely to suffer from depression
- Six times more likely to suffer from ADHD
- Three times more likely to suffer from substance use disorder
- Ten times more likely to suffer from bipolar disorder
- Twice more likely to have suicidal thoughts

With this shocking discovery, it is interesting that this topic is not trending news. This guide was made to highlight the psychological issues that arise with starting a business, and maintaining and thriving said business. In essence, the addressed or unaddressed mental health issues of entrepreneurs can impact their success. Many people try to push themselves to achieve their big goals, but never pause to address the reality of what could be holding them back. Sometimes, entrepreneurs feel stuck - and even believe they are stuck - because they don't have enough time to complete tasks, or because they procrastinate, or because they believe that their skills and abilities are not good enough for them to be successful. These beliefs may merely be a cover for unresolved trauma or mental health illness (anxiety, depression, etc.).

Business Self-Esteem is the foundation required in order for you to have a clear vision in the purpose of your business. It is the mental muscle of the business, and it is needed for it to thrive. Business Self-Esteem has to do with the entrepreneur and the business environment (structure, services, customers, networks, finances, etc.). If the entrepreneur does not feel good about their abilities and limits, they would have little value on opinions and ideas. Thus, the business will be limited and consequently, will not succeed. The customers will not believe in the service, finances will not be sustained and the networks will not interact. Entrepreneurs need to feel good about themselves and see themselves as deserving of the respect of others.

The aim of this journal is to teach you how to change your mindset, in order to attract success.

About An Entrepreneurial Therapy Guide to Overcome Self-Doubt

This journal is **not** therapy; however, it can guide you to identify concerns - with respect to your spiritual, mental, emotional, and physical well-being - that keep you from having a successful business. This guided journal will help you find appropriate resources and help you advocate for help in areas where you're lacking in. The aim of this guided journal is to help create your self-care plan by identifying negative thoughts, help learn to manage stress, improve vibrations, and enhance your relationships with others.

Business Self-Esteem is introduced in this journal, in a bid for you to learn a systemic approach to analyzing your mental health, and also discover how your mental health determines the success of your business as a whole. This journal will dig deeper in the meaning in the self-esteem section.

Journaling can be easy, fun and relaxing. There are so many therapeutic benefits to journaling; it has been found to create order when your world feels chaotic, and it also allows you to explore the 'why' behind your feelings instead of holding on to your negative thoughts. This therapy guide journal has journaling prompts, affirmations and information specifically for entrepreneurs. Journaling will help to calm and clear your mind in order for you to be motivated enough to reach your full potential in your business.

An entrepreneurial therapy guide to overcome self-doubt will do the following:

1. Improve your self-esteem
    a. This journal gives you affirmations and worksheets to increase your entrepreneurial self-esteem.
    b. This journal teaches the importance of self-care.
2. Improve your time management
    a. You will learn the importance of time management and how it can impact your productivity and well-being.
3. Identify your mental health needs
    a. Here, you will know what you need in order to have clarity for the sake of your mental health.
    b. You will also find out the difference between coaching and therapy, and how they can work for you.
4. Improve your relationships with others
    a. This journal will teach you to establish and reestablish healthy relationships.

5. Help you set and achieve your goals
    a. This helps you monitor your progress and feel motivated enough to continue to focus on your success.
    b. SMART goal-setting.
6. Keep track of your ideas
    a. It is great to have a place where you can record all your ideas in one place anytime and anywhere. Whenever an idea comes to mind, you can journal it and revisit it when you can.
7. Relieve stress
    a. Having a place to reflect and write down your feelings helps you to "brain dump" or "schedule stress" that you have accumulated over time.
8. Boost your memory
    a. Science shows that our brains make stronger connections with the information we have learnt after we write them down to recall in the future. This information journal teaches emotional intelligence and gives you space to allow brain connection.
9. Inspire creativity
    a. Journaling is the best way to explore your internal creativity. This is your journal, so, write down anything that comes to mind. Let your imagination take you on a journey of getting to know the inner depths of your creativity.

Throughout this journal you will see butterflies as a reminder of your transformation. Butterflies symbolize one of the most iconic examples of transformation in nature. A butterfly often appears when someone is going through tough times, as a symbol of support-a lightness of being.

“

I choose prosperity over failure.

”

Motivation

Intrinsic (internal) Motivation Vs. Extrinsic (external) Motivation

In the beginning stages of creating your own business, naturally, you would be pumped with thoughts that your idea is amazing. When your idea starts to grow into a plan, you then start to feel mixed emotions. These emotions will most likely range from excitement, fear, happiness, doubts, overwhelm, content and many more, through the course of planning. What isn't often discussed is how these emotions can alter your desire to complete tasks. With positive emotions, people tend to be motivated to complete projects; however, when the emotions do not feel good, people tend to have lower motivation to complete tasks. It is important to find and maintain motivation in business. For success and clarity in what you are doing, you need to identify *why* you want a business and understand the risks you will be taking. Intrinsic motivation involves performing a task because it's personally rewarding to you.

Internal motivators include all the internal reasons why you want to create and do well in your business. This involves emotions that motivate you to want success.

As an entrepreneur, one of the most important motivators for success is receiving positive feedback from clients or the community; it really helps to increase motivation. Positive feedback is important, and should be demonstrated to your customers by you reminding customers to write testimonials, write reviews and share your business on social media.

How do you encourage your clients to write testimonials and reviews on social media?

Here are tips:

Simply ask — write it in a 'thank you' note.

Explain why reviews are important.

Make writing a review as simple as possible.

*Create multiple space*s to leave reviews.

This feedback assures and encourages you, as the entrepreneur, of the success of your product or services.

Pride: Pride in yourself and your work can be a powerful motivator for many.
What are you proud of in your business?

Passion: Does love for what you do give you the drive to be able to work through the challenges?

Challenges: Do you thrive on challenges? Do you purposefully take on initiatives that will stretch you and provide learning opportunities?

External motivations involve completing a task or exhibiting a behavior because of outside causes; these causes can include avoiding punishment or receiving a reward.
The external motivators are people, places, and things that motivate us to want more in our lives. They help us to understand why our business needs to be structured. Here are external reasons why people are motivated to have successful businesses.

Money: Is wealth, paying off debts or living luxuriously a motivator for you?

Society: Are you driven by the desire to solve a common problem or improve the lives of others?

Family: Is the idea of passing down a successful business important to you? Are you building a legacy you can pass down to your children? Are you starting a business to support or honor your family in some way?

Knowing your motivation gives you clarity, and you will be less likely to lose your focus, get pulled off-track, and forget why you embarked on this journey in the first place.
When you understand your motivation and use it, you will have the confidence it takes to make the decisions you need to make when starting your business.

Intrinsic

Make a list of things that drive you from the inside in the left column. For each item in the left column, write your motivators in the right column.

What is your inner drive that propels you?	Motivators
E.g. fun	*E.g. planning events*

Intrinsic

Make a list of things that drive you from the inside in the left column. For each item in the left column, write your motivators in the right column.

What is your inner drive that propels you?	Motivators
E.g. fun	E.g. planning events

Questions To Enhance Your Motivation

What are your expectations as a business owner? Visualize your business being successful.

Are you afraid of what may happen if you don't start a business and or become successful?

Do you look at your business to solidify your credibility or establish yourself as an expert?

“*Everything is always working out for me.*”

SMART Goals

"A goal is a dream with a deadline."

Without clear goals, you will not have a solid direction on where you're headed in life.
When running a business, goals can help take your business to the next level.

Setting goals and meeting them is a great way for an entrepreneur to see their business thrive. Goals help you to stay organized and are a big part of self-care. SMART Goals are a great way to measure your accomplishments.

S: Specific	**Be very descriptive/specific about what your desired outcome is going to look like**
M: Measurable	**You should be able to track your progress and measure your success**
A: Attainable	**Call it what you like, but your goals should be ones that you could reasonably achieve**
R: Realistic	**Make sure you can realistically reach your goals without becoming a workaholic or have relationship struggles**
T: Timed	**Have a stopping point, so your success can be measured over a finite period of time**

SMART Goals

Setting realistic and achievable outcomes

My goal is:

S: Specific	What do I want to happen?	
M: Measurable	How will I know when I have achieved my goal?	
A: Attainable	Is the goal realistic and how will I accomplish it?	
R: Realistic	Why is my goal important to me?	
T: Timed	What is my deadline for this goal?	

SMART Goals

Setting realistic and achievable outcomes

My goal is:		
S: Specific	What do I want to happen?	
M: Measurable	How will I know when I have achieved my goal?	
A: Attainable	Is the goal realistic and how will I accomplish it?	
R: Realistic	Why is my goal important to me?	
T: Timed	What is my deadline for this goal?	

“*I say yes to myself.*”

Business Self-Esteem

What is self-esteem?

Having good self-esteem wavers from time to time, due to life's obstacles and is normal behavior. If an entrepreneur can easily adjust to changes without giving up, it is a good sign that they are resilient. Resilience is the capacity to recover from difficulties, toughness and trauma quickly.

Self-esteem involves how we value and perceive ourselves. When you view yourself in the mirror, what do you see? Typically, what we see when we assess our reflection in the mirror is based on our opinions and beliefs about ourselves.

What is Business Self-Esteem?

It is the mental muscle of the business that makes it thrive. Business Self-Esteem includes the entrepreneur and the business environment (structure, services, customers, networks, finances, etc.). If the entrepreneur does not feel good about their abilities and limits, they would have little value on opinions and ideas.

Do you believe you will have a successful business?

Having self-confidence in yourself will help your business prosper. Your confidence becomes part of your business because it shows up in everything you do. Having good self-esteem about your business means you have high confidence in your own ability and that you are willing to take responsible risks. Business confidence and self-confidence will help you overcome adversity. Self-esteem is important as an entrepreneur, particularly because of the benefits of confidence.

Confidence breeds Success

"Confidence is contagious. So is lack of confidence."

When you are confident, people will have no choice but to listen to what you have to say. They will want to be around you and will buy into your business.

People want to be around successful, confident people. They want to network with you because they believe you have knowledge or know people who have knowledge. You will make solid decisions in your business and you should easily adjust to change when needed.

Here are tips to boosting entrepreneurial self-esteem:

- Set goals that are easy to achieve. You will achieve this by using the SMART goal technique found on page 11
- Utilize daily affirmations and journaling found throughout this journal
- Have a support network
- Represent your brand by wearing it, sharing what you do with others and getting involved in the community under your business name

As you assess your business self-esteem, start with your own self-esteem. For most people, their low confidence may come from the negative thoughts that come up.

Negative thoughts about ourselves can come up from time to time. But what's important is that when we identify these thoughts, we try to change them, and in turn, impact our growth mindset. Allow this journal to guide you to change your thoughts. Learn about yourself in order to make changes. Change does not occur overnight, and so, challenging these negative thoughts one day at a time is very important. The way we view our behaviors, ourselves, and the world around us can feel difficult to change, but if we take small steps, we will achieve it.

Successful Entrepreneurs Have Growth Mindset

Carol Dweck's book, Mindset, explains her research between Growth Mindset vs. Fixed Mindset. An entrepreneur with a "growth" mindset is able to learn from mistakes and use them to "grow" their business, whereas, those with a fixed mindset might dwell on failures and see setbacks as a reason to give up.

The difference between Growth and Fixed mindset helps us understand how we view our potential.
A **fixed mindset** is "the belief that an individual's basic abilities, intelligence, talents and skills are fixed traits."

As a successful entrepreneur, you want to strive for a growth mindset.

A **growth mindset** is "the belief that an individual's most basic abilities and skills can be developed through determination, dedication and hard work—brains and talent are just the starting point."
Here are ways to incorporate a growth mindset in your business:

1. Make accountability your company's culture
    - Be responsible and accept accountability
    - Listen to criticism — it can greatly improve your business.
2. Don't focus on your failures
    - Things happen; move forward and learn from the failures
    - Know that setbacks happen and continue to power them
3. Work hard
    - Put in the work through time and effort
    - Make sure you ask for help and know when to help others
4. Do what you LOVE for people who LOVE what you do
    - Know your **Niche**

This is when you find the very specific activity or position that sets you apart from everyone else, and in which you can find success or fulfillment. Marketing is easier with a niche and protects you from burnout because you are connected with those that better match your skill or product.

Journal Entry

"Discovering your Purpose is as Important as Finding your Niche."

When you're able to answer the questions below, you will bring much more value and expertise to those that need you.

"When you love what you do, you have fun delivering your products and or services."

What are you knowledgeable about?

What do you love to do?

CHOOSE YOUR NICHE

Do you know how to attract "YOUR" clients?
Try here...

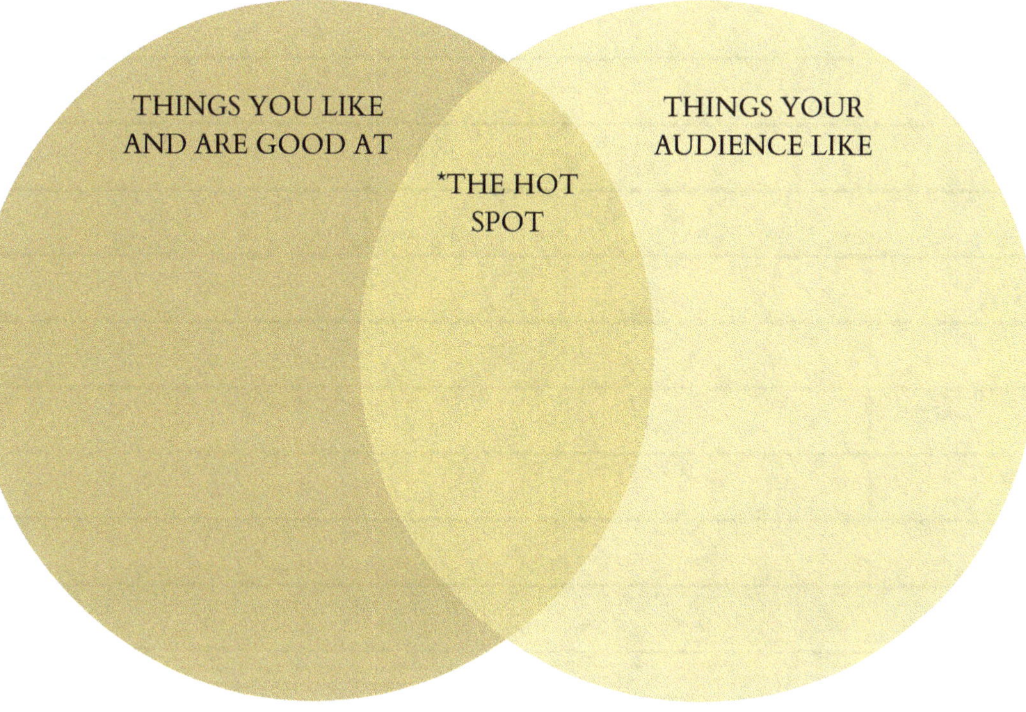

***The Hot Spot = Your Niche**

Growth Mindset

Use this worksheet to list your ideas

IDEA

PLAN

REFLECTION

MINDSET LANGUAGE

Flip your thinking! We strive for a Growth Mindset. Use these when you feel stuck. When you struggle to make a sound decision. Complete the speech bubbles:

Instead of:	**Say:**
I am not good with money.	
I can't do this!	
The market is over saturated. No one wants what I have to offer!	

GROWTH MINDSET

Grow your thinking! Complete the speech bubbles:

Mistakes you made in your business.

How will your mistakes grow your business?

Negative Thinking- Cognitive Distortions

Psychiatrist, Aaron Beck, invented Cognitive Behavioral Therapy (CBT). He discovered that people have negative ideas about themselves ("I am not worth anything"), about the world ("Everybody hates me") or about the future ("There are no hopes for my future"). Numerous research studies suggest that CBT leads to significant improvement in functioning and quality of life. In many studies, CBT has been demonstrated to be as effective as, or more effective than, other forms of psychological therapy or psychiatric medications.

Negative thoughts impact what we do and don't do.

How we identify and get rid of negative thoughts is to track them. We can't change behavior if we don't realize how bad it is. Here is a thought tracker and other worksheets that can help you identify negative thoughts about yourself and others.

DATE:

Reframe your thoughts:
Write down every negative and self-limiting thoughts that you may believe about yourself and transform them into positive thoughts.

NEGATIVE THOUGHTS	POSITIVE THOUGHTS

DATE:

THOUGHT TRACKER

Reframe your thoughts:
Write down every negative and self-limiting thoughts that you may believe about yourself
and transform them into positive thoughts.

NEGATIVE THOUGHTS	POSITIVE THOUGHTS

DATE:

Reframe your thoughts:
Write down every negative and self-limiting thoughts that you may believe about yourself
and transform them into positive thoughts.

NEGATIVE THOUGHTS	POSITIVE THOUGHTS

Negative → Positive

MY NEGATIVE THOUGHT:

Evidence for my thought:

Evidence against my thought:

How can I reframe my negative thought to a more realistic one?

Imposter Syndrome

Imposter Syndrome is an experience and NOT a mental illness. However, it is not good for your mental health. This syndrome is not recognized in the diagnostic manual (book used to diagnose mental illness); however, it is a popular trending topic. This thinking can lead to mental illnesses such as anxiety or depression. Imposter Syndrome is when you don't believe that your success is deserved. When you have this syndrome, you may feel like your friends or colleagues are going to discover you're a fraud because you don't deserve your job and accomplishments. The root cause of these thoughts is not consistent and can stem from anywhere, but oftentimes, it can come as a result of people's internalized feelings from their past; the feeling of, "In order to be loved or be lovable, I need to achieve."

The Imposter Syndrome can manifest itself in the following ways:

1. "I am only here because I got lucky and I know they know."
   - This is the, I am an imposter (fraud) thinking
2. "My education or years of experience is not good enough."
   - This is you doubting your abilities, when you have all the abilities that currently contribute to your success
3. "Was my work really worth this much money?"
   - This is you doubting your worth when you put in the work
4. "I am not worthy of all this attention."
   - This is your self-esteem issue interfering with how people view your great work
5. "My experience is lacking."
   - This is you doubting the power of your abilities
6. Here are a few characteristics of Imposter Syndrome:
   - Lack of self-confidence
   - Feelings of inadequacy
   - Self-doubt
   - Constant comparison to one another
   - Distrust in one's own intuition and capabilities
   - Negative self-talk
   - Dwelling in the past
   - Anxiety
   - Constant comparison to other people

How to Deal with Imposter Syndrome:

Name it.

Identify when imposter syndrome arrives and then name it. Naming the feeling. helps you to move to the next step of challenging it.

Challenge it

Challenge your feelings. You can do this by journaling it or utilizing the thought tracker.

Create an accomplishment list

We should all have a list where we track all our accomplishments. If you do not have an accomplishment list, start making one as soon as possible. This sheet will be handy when you doubt your abilities. It is common to forget our accomplishments — big or small, but this list helps remind you of how powerful, successful and smart you are.

Measure Your Progress

By celebrating small wins like your 1st sale/customer or 100 days in business. Put your short-term goals into smaller tasks by using SMART goals.

Find an Accountability Partner or a Network of Entrepreneurs

If you are struggling to reach goals, or feel lonely in the entrepreneurship world, engage with people. The support structure is impactful, especially when it comes to mental health. Take care of your mental health by surrounding yourself with the right kind of people.

Having an accountability partner is like a partnership, where you mutually agree to coach each other and provide feedback on a regular basis. With an accountability partner, you each agree to talk daily or weekly through feedback sessions, where you share wins and talk about your current challenges. They hold you accountable for completing your goals.

The following page is the **Clance IP Scale.** The Impostor Test was developed to help individuals determine whether or not they have IP characteristics and, if so, to what extent

Clance IP Scale

For each question, please circle the number that best indicates how true the statement is of you. It is best to give the
the first response that enters your mind rather than dwelling on each statement and thinking about it over and over.

1. I have often succeeded on a test or task even though I was afraid that I would not do well before I undertook the task.

1	2	3	4	5
NOT AT ALL TRUE	RARELY	SOMETIMES	OFTEN	VERY TRUE

2. I can give the impression that I'm more competent than I really am.

1	2	3	4	5
NOT AT ALL TRUE	RARELY	SOMETIMES	OFTEN	VERY TRUE

3. I avoid evaluations if possible and have a dread of others evaluating me.

1	2	3	4	5
NOT AT ALL TRUE	RARELY	SOMETIMES	OFTEN	VERY TRUE

4. When people praise me for something I've accomplished, I'm afraid I won't be able to live up to their expectations of

1	2	3	4	5
NOT AT ALL TRUE	RARELY	SOMETIMES	OFTEN	VERY TRUE

5. I sometimes think I obtained my present position or gained my present success because I happened to be in the right place at the right time or knew the right people.

1	2	3	4	5
NOT AT ALL TRUE	RARELY	SOMETIMES	OFTEN	VERY TRUE

6. I'm afraid people important to me may find out that I'm not as capable as they think I am.

1	2	3	4	5
NOT AT ALL TRUE	RARELY	SOMETIMES	OFTEN	VERY TRUE

7. I tend to remember the incidents in which I have not done my best more than those times I have done my best

1	2	3	4	5
NOT AT ALL TRUE	RARELY	SOMETIMES	OFTEN	VERY TRUE

8. I rarely do a project or task as well as I'd like to do it.

1	2	3	4	5
NOT AT ALL TRUE	RARELY	SOMETIMES	OFTEN	VERY TRUE

9. Sometimes I feel or believe that my success in my life or in my job has been the result of some kind of error.

1	2	3	4	5
NOT AT ALL TRUE	RARELY	SOMETIMES	OFTEN	VERY TRUE

10. It's hard for me to accept compliments or praise about my intelligence or accomplishments.

1	2	3	4	5
NOT AT ALL TRUE	RARELY	SOMETIMES	OFTEN	VERY TRUE

11. At times, I feel my success has been due to some kind of luck.

1	2	3	4	5
NOT AT ALL TRUE	RARELY	SOMETIMES	OFTEN	VERY TRUE

12. I'm disappointed at times in my present accomplishments and think I should have accomplished much more.

1	2	3	4	5
NOT AT ALL TRUE	RARELY	SOMETIMES	OFTEN	VERY TRUE

13. Sometimes I'm afraid others will discover how much knowledge or ability I really lack.

1	2	3	4	5
NOT AT ALL TRUE	RARELY	SOMETIMES	OFTEN	VERY TRUE

14. I'm often afraid that I may fail at a new assignment or undertaking even though I generally do well at what I attempt.

1	2	3	4	5
NOT AT ALL TRUE	RARELY	SOMETIMES	OFTEN	VERY TRUE

15. When I've succeeded at something and received recognition for my accomplishments, I have doubts that I can keep repeating that success.

1	2	3	4	5
NOT AT ALL TRUE	RARELY	SOMETIMES	OFTEN	VERY TRUE

16. If I receive a great deal of praise and recognition for something I've accomplished, I tend to discount the importance of what I've done.

1	2	3	4	5
NOT AT ALL TRUE	RARELY	SOMETIMES	OFTEN	VERY TRUE

17. I often compare my ability to those around me and think they may be more intelligent than I am.

1	2	3	4	5
NOT AT ALL TRUE	RARELY	SOMETIMES	OFTEN	VERY TRUE

18. I often worry about not succeeding with a project or examination, even though others around me have considerable confidence that I will do well.

1	2	3	4	5
NOT AT ALL TRUE	RARELY	SOMETIMES	OFTEN	VERY TRUE

19. If I'm going to receive a promotion or gain recognition of some kind, I hesitate to tell others until it is an accomplished fact.

1	2	3	4	5
NOT AT ALL TRUE	RARELY	SOMETIMES	OFTEN	VERY TRUE

20. I feel bad and discouraged if I'm not "the best" or at least "very special" in situations that involve achievement.

1	2	3	4	5
NOT AT ALL TRUE	RARELY	SOMETIMES	OFTEN	VERY TRUE

Scoring the Impostor Test

The Impostor Test was developed to help individuals determine whether or not they have IP characteristics and, if so, to what extent they are suffering.

After taking the Impostor Test, add together the numbers of the responses to each statement. If the total score is 40 or less, the respondent has few Impostor characteristics; if the score is between 41 and 60, the respondent has moderate IP experiences; A score between 61 and 80 means the respondent frequently has Impostor feelings; and a score higher than 80 means the respondent often has intense IP experiences. The higher the score, the more frequently and seriously the Impostor Phenomenon interferes in a person's life.

What to do with your score?

The score is to bring your attention to your thoughts. The following chart helps you address Imposter Syndrome:

Imposter Syndrome

Imposter Syndrome

01
Name it: Acknowledge your feelings and try to name those emotions.

02
Find out why you are feeling like this? Journal your thoughts

03
Challenge It! Obtain support through networking, accountability partner, coach or therapist.

04
Work on dismantling your thoughts. Use positive affirmations.

05
Create an Accomplishment List or Board. Hang it where you can see it. Prove to yourself why your negative thoughts are not true.

06
Create SMART goals and measure your progress.

Scarcity Mindset

"The mind is everything. What you think, you become."

Someone with a scarcity mindset believes that opportunities are few and far between, and that the accomplishments of others directly translate to personal failings in themselves.

People with scarcity mindset may think:

"There are no good opportunities to advance in the world, as **all** of the 'good' opportunities have been taken, and there's nothing left for me."

"Why should I create this business? I will never reach the levels of success as those who have the same business."

A scarcity mentality is what hinders many of us from achieving our goals.

A scarcity mindset is when you are so obsessed with a lack of something (time or money), and you can't seem to focus on anything else, no matter how hard you try.

Focusing on something you don't have can take a toll on your mental health. You can get "tunnel vision" when all you think about is the unmet need.

All entrepreneurs should strive for an **abundance** mentality; a mentality that make it easy to believe that there is plenty for everyone.

Scarcity mentality isn't a personality trait. It is the things around you, especially your thoughts, which bring it on. Such things include:

- Believing that situations are permanent
- Believing that life's situations are fixed

–these thoughts deplete our energy, harms our self-esteem, and makes life complex. Nothing in life is permanent.

An abundant mentality sees life as an adventure, even in situations that can trigger uncertainty.

Remember, it's normal to have negative thoughts from time to time. It's important to understand that thoughts and words are important, only if they're helpful to us. When negative thoughts arise, become an observer (observe and make note), and refuse to engage them. Do not allow the negative thoughts to manifest into words that we tell ourselves or anyone else.

Another topic that breeds the scarcity mindset is feeling envious towards others. It kills gratitude and fuels the fire of scarcity. Envy or jealousy does nothing to better our personal circumstances in any way.

Have you ever felt envious?

Is it because people APPEAR to be doing better than you in certain areas of their lives? So, what if they are?

Things they achieve can all be achieved by you as well, but they're only achievable if the mindset of scarcity is replaced with a different kind of thinking.... Think in abundance.

Social media can fuel negative thoughts of jealousy. If you find that you are having this kind of mindset, try a social media break.

When it comes to bettering our circumstances, we can consciously choose to dictate our time and energy towards doing so, and not wasting it on envious thoughts and feelings.

Daily Business Affirmations

I choose faith over fear

I have the power to create change

I believe in myself

I am worthy of acceptance

I choose to let go of everyone and everything that no longer serve me

I am a gracious giver and receiver

I am worthy of the success coming my way

My journey is my journey, and I will not compare my journey to others

My past mistakes do not define me, but they have helped me grow

I will ask for help and support when needed

My work makes a difference

My business is a huge success

I believe in myself and trust in my abilities to succeed in all that I do

Being successful is natural for me

I attract my ideal clients and customers with my energy

I create wonderful business opportunities every day

I love the freedom my business produces for me

Being my own boss is a responsibility I handle with care

People love what I do; they love my products and my services

I make good decisions

Daily Business Affirmations

I choose prosperity over failure

Everything is always working out for me

I say yes to myself

I invest money wisely

My mental and physical health are my priority

I am now creating my life exactly how I want it

I am stepping into the most successful time of my life

Sometimes, I will have bad days and that is ok

The feeling of overwhelm is a feeling that will pass when I breathe

I can achieve any goal that I set for myself

My income is constantly increasing

I am confident in my brand and mission

I am proud of myself and all I have accomplished

Negative thoughts have no power over me

I choose not to criticize myself or others

I am the definition of prosperity

I am not my mistakes

The Power of Words

Affirmations work like exercise, but for our minds; an intentional exercise that gets us to look at things in a positive way. Affirmations are positive statements that help us challenge our negative thoughts and/or self-sabotaging behavior, especially in situations where we'd like to see positive changes take place in our lives. These might include times when we want to:

- Raise our confidence before presentations or important meetings
- Control negative feelings such as frustration, anger, or impatience
- Improve our self-esteem
- Finish projects we've started
- Improve our productivity
- Overcome a bad habit

How to Write an Affirmation Statement

1. Think of a specific area, behavior, or belief that you struggle with

2. Think about the areas of your life that you'd like to change
Write down several areas or behaviors that you'd like to work on. Be sure that they are compatible with your core values.

3. Turn negatives into positives. If you are struggling with negative self-talk, note down the persistent thoughts or beliefs that bother you

4. Write your affirmation in the present tense
Write and speak your affirmation as if it's already happening. This helps you to believe that the statement is true right now.

5. Say it with emotion, like you mean it
Affirmations can be more effective when they carry emotional weight. You need to want this change to happen, so, every affirmation that you choose to repeat should be a phrase that's meaningful to you.

Write Your Own Affirmation

Things That Impact an Entrepreneur's Well-Being

Multitasking

The ability to multitask is something a lot of entrepreneurs and professionals wear as a badge of honor. But like Travis Bradberry notes in Forbes, numerous studies have shown that multitasking actually reduces workday productivity.
Ironically, the participants in the study who declared themselves effective multitaskers were the ones most likely to be the slowest at switching from one task to another. Remember, as thriving entrepreneur's, we want to be mindful in our work day.

Unhealthy Diet

As entrepreneurs, we are always on the go, and so, finding healthy food can be impossible, particularly when there are time constraints. What we can do to avoid this is to try to meal-prep before the busy week begins. Also, we can try to have healthy snacks that include fruits and vegetables in our workspace. Stay hydrated! "Drink Water and Mind My Business".

A paper in the British Journal of Health Psychology studied the effects of eating fruits and vegetables and found that the participants who ate the most fruits and veggies throughout the day reported higher levels of creativity, engagement, and focus.

Messy Workspace

Clutter can slow you down.
In a study reported in Harvard Business Review, people seated at messy desks took longer to answer word and color-matching questions than those at a tidy workspace.
When mess surrounds you, your sense of personal control is lessened, which makes it more difficult to self-regulate and complete your tasks.

Lack of preparation

Maintaining workday productivity means making sure that you have the tools required to accomplish your task.

Why is Self-Care Important as an Entrepreneur?

The self-care diagram creates a visual of what we should be doing to care for ourselves on a daily basis. Doing is the care in self-care. What are you doing for your self-care?

Self-Care benefits entrepreneurs in many ways. The hustle of an entrepreneur is a common theme in American culture. We tend to celebrate and reward the hustle mentality, but not praise great mental health care. The results of not taking care of our health are documented as high stress, burnout, health problems and lack of mental health care. Self-care benefits the entrepreneur by making life easier to balance, improving mental health and improving relationships.

IT IMPROVES CLARITY AND CREATIVITY

A calm mind is a clear mind, which allows for more creativity and inspiration to hit. If you are overwhelmed and trying to multitask by doing a million things at once, you won't be in the best state of mind to be creative, organized, and successful in your goals.

IT REDUCES STRESS LEVELS

Stress is a normal physical and emotional response to a threatening or overwhelming task/situation but it can have major consequences if not managed properly. As entrepreneurs, stress will inevitably play a role in our lives, so learning how to deal with it is very important. This is where self-care comes in; it works to activate the body's relaxation response by reducing cortisol and adrenaline levels in our bodies, which helps to reduce stress!

IT BOOSTS PRODUCTIVITY

A lot of research supports the idea that taking breaks and practicing self-care improve productivity. Even when you are super busy, 10 minutes away from your computer to practice some breathing, stretches, meditations or go for a walk can do wonders!

IT IMPROVES MENTAL HEALTH

One of the biggest contributions to mental health problems is stress. The psychological, emotional, and physical effects of prolonged and severe stress can be concerning, so, taking the time to prioritize your self-care is vital.

"I am now creating my life exactly how I want it."

7 Areas of Self-Care

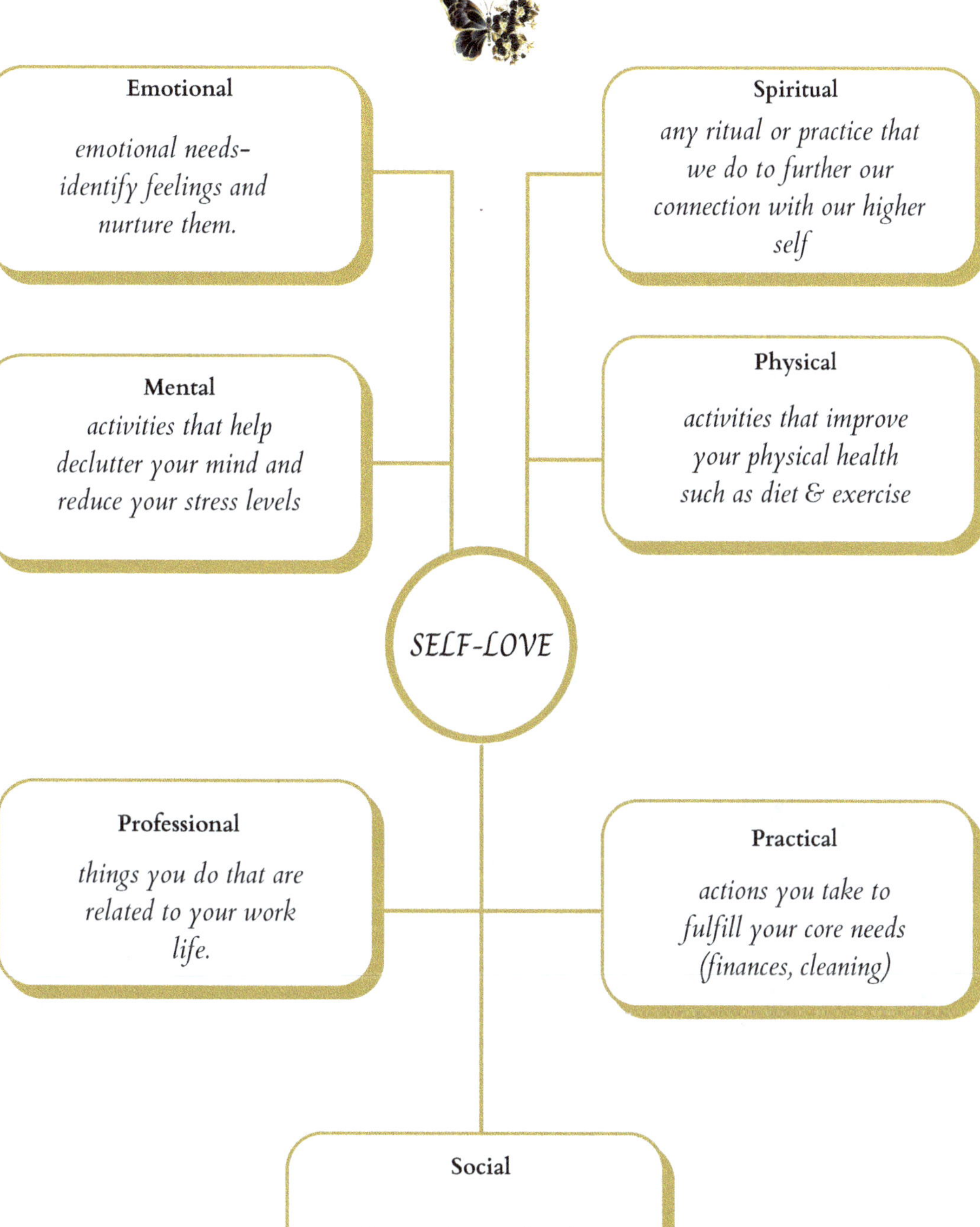

7 Areas of Self-Care

Write what you will do to take care of these areas

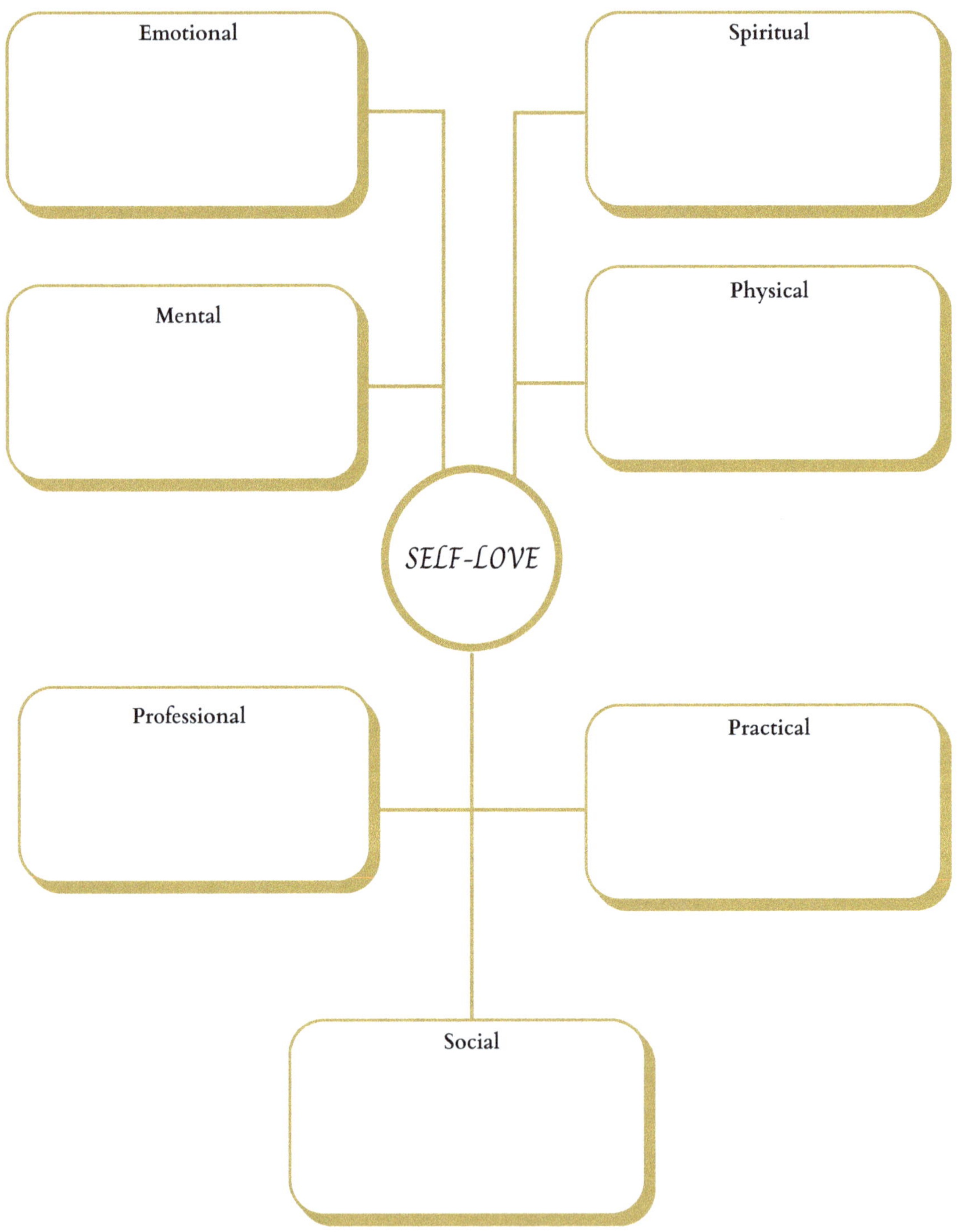

7 Areas of Self-Care

Write what you will do to take care of these areas

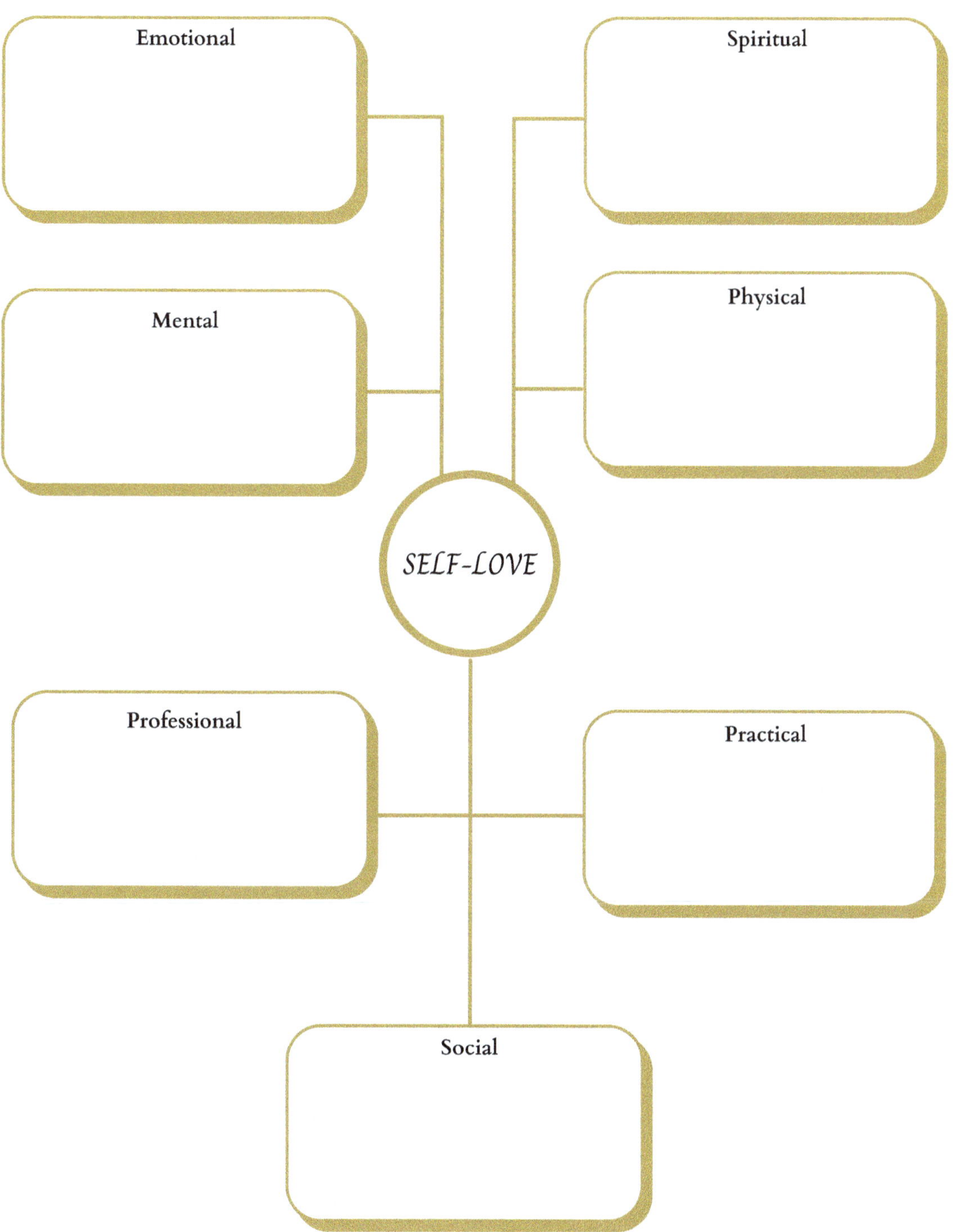

Self Love

IN THE SPACES BELOW, LIST ALL THE WAYS YOU CAN SHOW LOVE AND APPRECIATION TO YOURSELF

live
laugh
love

enjoy
every
moment.

DATE:

I'm happiest when I...

I'm unhappy when I...

WHAT DO I NEED TO DO TO MAKE THIS HAPPEN?

WHAT MAKES YOU UNHAPPY

I DEFINE MY OWN HAPPINESS.

2 THINGS THAT MAKE ME LAUGH...

3 THINGS THAT INSTANTLY PUT ME IN A GREAT MOOD:

DATE:

I'm happiest when I...

I'm unhappy when I...

WHAT DO I NEED TO DO TO MAKE THIS HAPPEN?

WHAT MAKES YOU UNHAPPY

I DEFINE MY OWN HAPPINESS.

2 THINGS THAT MAKE ME LAUGH...

3 THINGS THAT INSTANTLY PUT ME IN A GREAT MOOD:

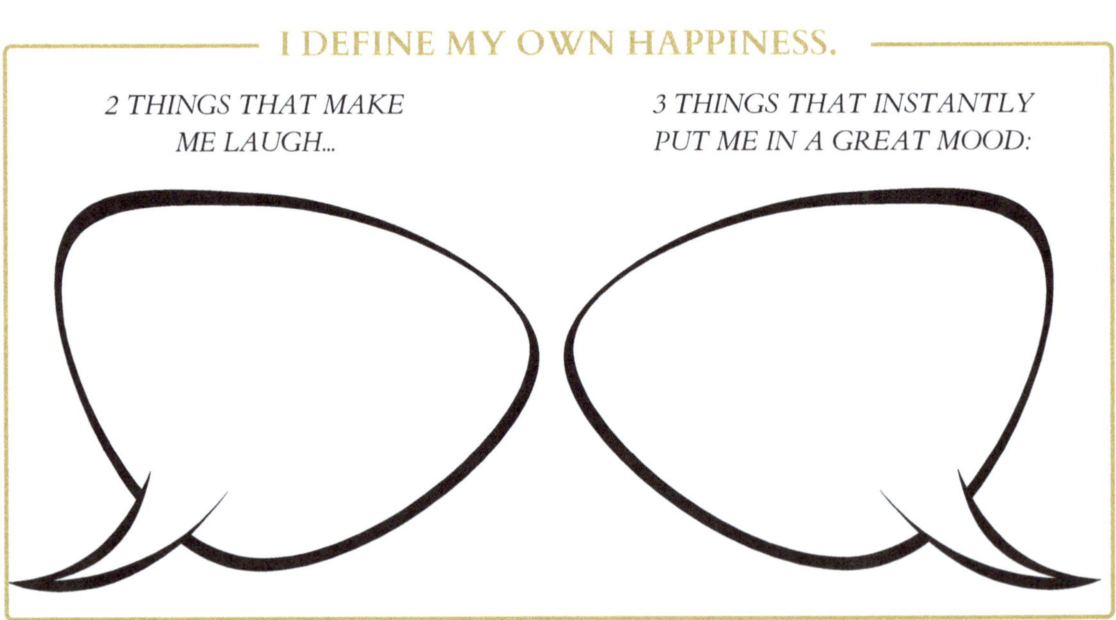

“

My mental and physical health are my priority.

”

Business Mindfulness

"Mindfulness means paying attention in a particular way: on purpose, in the present moment and nonjudgmentally."

Use mindfulness to improve your business.
Use these mindfulness tips to put you in a mindset that will help you work more effectively and efficiently, and thus, lead to higher productivity, better results and more satisfaction with your workdays.

What is it?

Mindfulness is something we all possess. However, we must tap into it in order to fully experience its true power. **Mindfulness is you focusing on being aware of what you're sensing and feeling in the moment.** It is intentional. Have you ever driven your vehicle and thought to yourself, "I don't remember driving here"? You have no recollection of driving to your destination. Or, you drive and don't know where you are going or where you are? It is definitely a scary situation to be in, but it is also one of the ways in which our bodies remind us that we need to focus on the present more. We need to learn how to be in the moment to safely and effectively complete tasks.

When we focus, we strive to do this **without interpretation or judgment.** This means we don't judge our thoughts that come up from focusing, and when we do, we redirect our focus back to the task at hand. If you are doing yoga, meditation, actively listening, or dancing, you focus on that task only.

Practicing mindfulness involves breathing methods, guided imagery, music, meditation, and other practices to relax the body and mind and help reduce stress.

Why It's Important to Use Mindfulness in your Business:

To Maintain Focus

There are so many tasks and day-to-day activities that come with having a business. If we do not focus on any task we have at hand, we find ourselves having incomplete tasks, disorganization, forgetfulness, and more things to do.

It changes your brain

The regular practice of mindfulness changes the neural structure of your brain. Cognitive Neuroscience research reports that mindfulness decreases the pathways in your brain responsible for mind wandering, while increasing the areas of the brain responsible for focus and attention. It will also decrease activity in the brain areas called the amygdala, leading to a decrease in stress and anxiety. Research also reports that practicing mindfulness increases the activity in the brain area responsible for positive moods.

Using mindfulness as a business owner, helps improve daily stressors by keeping focus to complete daily tasks and keeping an appropriate temperament under pressure.

Mindfulness keeps you disciplined

Being disciplined keeps you focused and task-oriented. If you do not have a schedule as an entrepreneur, it is harder to accomplish business success, have a purpose or reach goals. Having a trained mind can decrease doubt, leading you to business success.

Here Are Ways to Use Mindfulness in Your Business

Being mindful at work means taking the core elements of mindfulness, and incorporating it into your daily work habits. It means putting intention into your scheduling, tasks and processes.

Schedule your day mindfully & Plan your day.
Being mindful means being intentional about your thoughts and your actions. In order to effectively practice mindfulness as an entrepreneur, carefully think about how you spend your time and schedule your day.

Use a simple checklist. Using checklists to carry out complex tasks with many elements or steps to ensure consistency and efficiency. Write down your core daily activities that you need to complete, including work and personal activities. This helps create routine and structure through your day.

It's easier to relax and remain in touch with your thoughts when you know what is coming ahead of you. So, including even a tiny bit of structure in your day-to-day activities can help you be more mindful. Arranging and coordinating tasks and activities will make it easier to be focused.

Keep in mind that mindfulness and productivity work differently for everyone. If you're restless and energized in the morning, schedule meetings then.

Knowing and doing what's best for you is what being mindful is all about.

Start your workday by doing the most difficult task first.

If you - like most people - are more productive, attentive, and thoughtful in the morning, you can use that time to dive into your most difficult task of the day. Not only will you have the mental energy to drive you forward, but you will also knock out the toughest thing on your to-do list. Nothing else you need to do will feel quite as stressful, and so, the rest of your day will be more relaxing.

Take (and schedule) short breaks throughout the day. As you create your daily schedule, don't fill it with nonstop activity. Leave gaps in your schedule for breaks. In fact, schedule them in.

Plan time to leave your desk or office, and use that break to get away from your work, go for a walk, or practice mindfulness exercises.

Know when it's time to stop. The opposite of working mindfully is continuing to work to just pass time or fill a slot in your calendar. Stay in touch with your energy levels and productivity.

If you feel yourself starting to slip and just wasting time, stop working.
Even if it throws off your calendar, take a break to recharge, so you can return to do more efficient and effective work. And when it's the end of the day, stop.

The following strategies make you more productive, help you avoid distractions and stop you from mindlessly (and poorly) executing:

Make time for mindfulness exercises. Throughout the day, perform mindfulness exercises. These practices don't have to take much time. Spending even just a few minutes every hour can make a huge difference. Entrepreneurship is hard. You need every tool available to you to make it easier. So, remember, business tools aren't always directly tied to running everyday operations — sometimes, they are tools tied to helping you run your mind.

Breathe. Take a few deep inhalations. Hold your breath at the top of an inhale and after you exhale all the air.

Perform a body scan. Start at the top of your head and think about everything you feel moving all the way down to the tip of your toes.

Release tension. Stop and feel where you might be unintentionally holding tension in your body. Release tightness in your jaw, shoulders, or hands.

Stretch. Stand up and put your arms over your head and release the stress that might be building in your body.

Review all your senses. What do you smell, see, and hear? What can you touch and taste?

Observe your emotions and act accordingly. It's very difficult to be mindful and thoughtful when your emotions are running wild. So, practice paying attention to when you feel stressed, frustrated, tired, agitated, or hungry. Identify where you feel the emotion in your body, and question what event caused you to feel that way and why.

Be grateful. One of the best ways to reset your mindset is by spending a few moments in gratitude.

Morning Journal Entry: Stream of Consciousness

A way to relieve stress is to write in the stream of consciousness style first thing in the morning. This technique is called Morning pages. Julia Cameron's Book- 'The artist way' coined this idea.

When writing a morning page, you are just jotting down the first thoughts that come into your mind in the morning, no matter how senseless they sound.

In only 3 pages or less, write whatever comes to mind. It is highly recommended that this journaling exercise be done in the morning to start your day with less worry.

Mindful Monday

What does it mean to be mindful?

How can you practice being mindful every day in your business?

Sleep

Sleep and mental health are closely connected. Sleep deprivation affects your psychological state and mental health (Harvard Health Publishing, 2021).
After a night of tossing and turning, waking up in a crappy mood is pretty much the norm for people who work long hours. If you're predisposed to mental health conditions, bad sleep patterns could make your symptoms worse (Sleep Foundation, 2020).
Get enough sleep in order to be effective in your business and entrepreneurial decisions.
When you're running on fumes, you're less focused and more likely to make errors that you would have to go back to correct later.
You should be aiming for at least seven hours of sleep per night to be your best, most-effective self at work (Sleep Foundation, 2020).
Sleep is known to improve concentration and enhance problem-solving.

Here are ways to improve your sleep:

Schedule sleep
By carving out eight-plus hours on your calendar and sticking to it, you'll avoid over-committing, while affirming that sleep is a priority.

Monitor caffeine intake
Coffee could keep you up at night if you drink too much, especially late in the day, so, consider switching to decaf, herbal tea or water.

Exercise
Regular exercise can help you fall asleep quickly.

Blue screen blues
Do you check your phone, laptop or tablet before bed? If so, blue light may be suppressing your body's production of melatonin — a key hormone for sleep. Avoid screens two to three hours before bedtime and - to eliminate texting temptation - implement a no-phone policy in the bedroom.

Sleep Log

Month of:

DATE	HOURS OF SLEEP												ENERGY
DAY	1	2	3	4	5	6	7	8	9	10	11	12	★★★★★

Sleep Log

Month of:

DATE	HOURS OF SLEEP												ENERGY
DAY	1	2	3	4	5	6	7	8	9	10	11	12	★★★★★

Sleep Log

Month of:

DATE	HOURS OF SLEEP												ENERGY
DAY	1	2	3	4	5	6	7	8	9	10	11	12	★★★★★

“

Sometimes, I will have bad days and that is ok.

”

Entrepreneurs & Relationships

Relationships are key to an entrepreneur's success. New or aspiring entrepreneurs can enhance their chances of success by making sure they prioritize important relationships, while creating a thriving business. As a business owner, it is important to spend quality time with your family or friends. Even when we don't have a lot of time to spend, it is important that we make time to focus on our relationships, even if it is for one hour. One hour of attentive time in relationships is more impactful than three hours of time that is not meaningful or engaging.

Here are a few relationship dynamics that will help you improve your business:

Children

The most draining thing about being an entrepreneur is that you work at any time of the day, and your hours are usually longer. Unfortunately, you're more likely to not have paid days off. There are many times when you may struggle with making important events with your children or children who have an important role in your life. Here are ways you can do this:
Engage your children in activities that they like to do. For example: Play video games even if you don't have interest.
Switch up routines with your child. For example: If you usually don't pick your child up from school, do it.
Create mealtime rituals.
Have serious conversations in car rides about life, questions about their life, information about yours… they don't have to be long conversations.

Mentors

Most entrepreneurs are notoriously independent workers, but over time, they learn that some outside perspective can save them valuable time, energy, and money.
Finding a mentor who is willing to share their experience may be one of the most important differentiators between a business that doesn't do well and one that flourishes. Ideally, a mentor is someone farther down the road who has experienced failure and lived to talk about it. When considering a mentor, look for someone who:

- Will ask great questions to clarify focus, needs/goals, and resources
- Is willing to be vulnerable with their personal and professional life
- Is flexible and can match your schedule to meet at least once every other month
- Will listen to you more than talk

There are also peer boards and committees that provide some of these benefits, but many require revenue before joining.

Spouse/Life partner

When successful entrepreneurs are interviewed about their success, they often cite their partner for giving them courage and keeping priorities straight. Having a healthy relationship means that both partners have to communicate effectively and have patience.

Your home life should be a respite from the stresses of the world. Having a lasting relationship are "relationship goals" but you need to also invest in your relationship to ensure that if the business fails, you still have each other. No matter how supportive your spouse is of the business, many partners of entrepreneurs consider the start-up as "Bae." To avoid or reduce this, make sure to prioritize your relationship and regularly check-in together. Make it a practice, just as you would your business, to regularly review personal and business goals and intimate needs. Find ways to speak their love language.

"Preventative maintenance is easier than a blown-out engine."

Consider hiring a couples coach or counselor for your marriage; this doesn't mean there's a dire problem. Establishing a connection with a relationship coach or therapist might mean you only check in when needed. It also acknowledges that marriage takes individual and couples work to be successful.

Best friend- Accountability Partner/ Network Group

For an entrepreneur, having someone to listen when things are rough provides an additional source of support and affirmation. People can bring out the best in each other.

A *best friend* is someone other than your significant other that you do different activities with, just to blow off steam or do something that doesn't look anything like work. They can give you sound feedback and remind you about the importance of quality relationships.

Having an *accountability partner* helps keep you accountable of your professional and personal goals. They are not afraid to call you out of your comfort zone.

Networking is about sharing, not taking. Regularly engaging with your contacts and finding opportunities to assist them helps to strengthen the relationship.

Regularly attending professional and social events will help make your face and brand known. Learning experiences and goals is a key benefit for networking because it allows you to gain new insights that you may not have thought of. By continually putting yourself out there and meeting new people, you're effectively stepping outside your comfort zone and building invaluable social skills and self-confidence to build business self-esteem. The more you network, the more you'll grow and learn how to make lasting connections.

Surround yourself with people that will push to do and be better.

Healthy Relationships

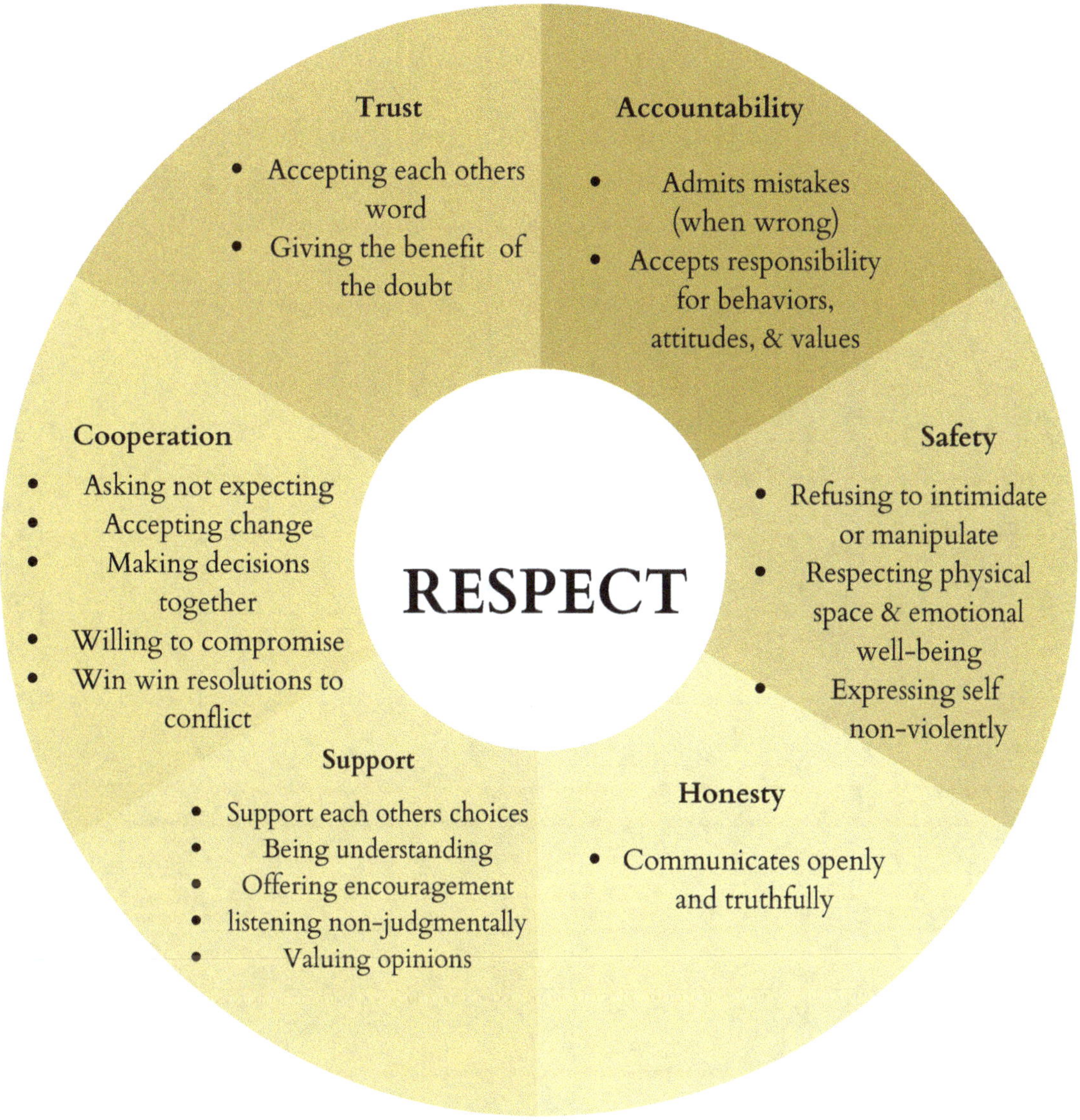

Trust

- Accepting each others word
- Giving the benefit of the doubt

Accountability

- Admits mistakes (when wrong)
- Accepts responsibility for behaviors, attitudes, & values

Cooperation

- Asking not expecting
- Accepting change
- Making decisions together
- Willing to compromise
- Win win resolutions to conflict

RESPECT

Safety

- Refusing to intimidate or manipulate
- Respecting physical space & emotional well-being
- Expressing self non-violently

Support

- Support each others choices
- Being understanding
- Offering encouragement
- listening non-judgmentally
- Valuing opinions

Honesty

- Communicates openly and truthfully

This diagram shows that relationships are healthy when everyone practice **respect**.

Feeling Ownership

When you have a conflict with someone, try this worksheet. Identify your emotions and the conflict. Complete the sentences to express your emotions:

I feel ______________________ when ______________________

____

I feel ______________________ when ______________________

____

I feel ______________________ when ______________________

____

I feel ______________________ when ______________________

____

I feel ______________________ when ______________________

____

Something I can do about this is ______________________

Feeling Ownership

When you have a conflict with someone, try this worksheet. Identify your emotions and the conflict. Complete the sentences to express your emotions:

I feel ______________________ when ______________________

____

I feel ______________________ when ______________________

____

I feel ______________________ when ______________________

____

I feel ______________________ when ______________________

____

I feel ______________________ when ______________________

____

Something I can do about this is ______________________

Identify Your Support System

Who are your role models, network, and support system in your life? Mention their qualities, abilities or strengths that led you to give them that role. Write down how they influence your actions, thinking patterns and behaviors.

Person (role models, network, support system)	Attributes	Influence on Me

Manifest- Law of Attraction

We bring what we attract to our lives. Manifesting is simply something that is put into your reality through thoughts, feelings and beliefs. Whatever you focus on is what you bring into reality, so you need to always speak positivity in your business. Manifesting is making a choice and acting on it. It is not just wishing and believing.

It is getting your thoughts, actions, and emotions to move as well. You can do this by journaling the thoughts of what you want, the actions you need to take and the kind of emotions that align with your positive thoughts. Some people struggle with identifying emotions. The Emotional Guidance Scale by Abraham Hicks is a great diagram to help learn your emotions.

When we dream of great things happening, we want the wording that we use to manifest to be precise. Journaling is one technique used to help you visualize what you are asking for. Know what you want by stating things as if you already have it. Here are tips to use when journaling your manifestations.

Define what you want and ask for it.
"What do you want?" This question focuses your mind and forces it to gain clarity. The law of attraction advises that you ask clearly, and not give mixed signals. If you are asking for something you don't really want, or something you don't fully believe is achievable, it's not going to happen.

Your request and behaviors must be consistent.
Practice by journaling, clearly asking what you want for yourself, business, family, or clients.

Positive Vibes Only
Expect the things you want, not the things you don't want. If you expect to face difficult challenges and toxic people, you are training your mind to notice adversity, and subconsciously attract them to you. Observe it and change your thought. You will rise to every challenge, and your work will make a difference.
Each day you wake up, choose whether you "have" to do something or you "get" to do something. You will use the day to get closer to your goals, and that is exactly what will happen. Make this process a habit.

Positive conversations attract positive people. Success attracts success. You can see it working on a basic level. If you are difficult to deal with, you will find yourself with clients who are too. You set the tone, and that determines the tone you get back.
A happy mindset attracts great things.

Find ways to stay positive by implementing good self-care practices like exercise and healthy eating. Use inspirational tools like music, videos and podcasts that give inspirational messages from other entrepreneurs who are doing better than you are.
Be Aware of Things that Lower Your Vibration. Remember, you want high positive Vibes.

Inspired Action

According to the law of attraction, there is a difference between "work" and "taking inspired action." Taking inspired action towards goals is effortless because you feel the strong inner urge to do it with purpose. Your purpose is filled with your desire to be successful. It is action that feels effortless, joyous and brings no stress. Inspired action leads you to the next successful step in your business.

Are you doing what makes you happy or are you doing what others are doing?

Believe in Abundance
Stop thinking that you must compete with other entrepreneurs. Everyone can win big and have different paths to success.
Energy spent on focusing on someone else is energy that could be spent on your own business.

Practice gratitude
The more you practice being grateful for specific components of your life, the more you will have to be grateful for.
Think of why you are grateful for the people in your business; that includes network. Being specific and telling those people will lead to more of the same behavior, which will in turn lead to having more to be grateful for. The ways in which people are valued forms part of their identity and aligns their actions even more strongly.

Reframe Time
Believing that you never have enough time to do anything will mean that you will never have enough time to do anything. Subconsciously, your actions will match that belief. Things will distract you, and you'll also allow yourself to be distracted. The law of attraction asserts that negative affirmations, such as "I don't have time" is highly damaging to your goals and growth mindset.

Tell yourself that you are an expert at managing your time. This will shift your mindset, and your actions will align with your belief.

Dream big
Picture having a million-dollar business!

“I am stepping into the most successful time of my life.”

Things That Lower Your Vibration

A **vibration** is a state of being, the atmosphere, or the energetic quality of a person, place, thought, or thing. Next to the 'low vibration words' write how they affect your well-being.

Fear
Negative Self-Talk
Limiting Yourself
Toxic Friends
Poor Diet
Toxic Friends
People-Pleasing
No Exercise
No Accountability
Greed
Ungratefulness
Fueling Drama
Constant Complaining

Manifest- Law Attraction

If you believe that a million-dollar business is unattainable or unrealistic, then it is just that. If you believe it's an amount you could never have, or aren't worthy of, your actions and your future will match that belief. Always value yourself higher. Choose to believe what you say and value your actions to create money, power, and profound impact.

Confidently state your price and believe with everything in you that your product and or service are worth every cent. Put forward more impressive and ambitious plans because you have belief in your capability to deliver them.
Believing in you, manifesting, and understanding the law of attraction will bring business success. You will be a thriving entrepreneur.

Believe Success is Inevitable
The law of attraction states that your higher power will help in making things that you feel are impossible happen. Think of the popular saying, "God makes a way out of no way."
Believing also involves acting like something is already yours. Acting like you have the multimillion-dollar company helps create a clear vision of your business goals, and then allows you step into an elevated version of yourself.

*3-6-9 Manifestation Techniques

Step 1. Create an affirmation for what you want to manifest. Be clear about what you want
Step 2. Write the Affirmations
3 times in the morning
6 times at noon
9 times before bedtime
Visualize your manifestation happening for 30 days
Stay dedicated - Put in the work by staying focused on your goal.

3-6-9 Manifestation Techniques

Step 1. Create an affirmation for what you want to manifest. Be clear about what you want.

Step 2. Write the Affirmations.

3 times in the morning.

6 times at noon.

9 times before bedtime.

Visualize your manifestation happening for 30 days.
Stay dedicated - Put in the work by staying focused on your goal.

3-6-9 Manifestation Techniques

Step 1. Create an affirmation for what you want to manifest. Be clear about what you want.

Step 2. Write the Affirmations.

3 times in the morning.

6 times at noon.

9 times before bedtime.

Visualize your manifestation happening for 30 days.
Stay dedicated - Put in the work by staying focused on your goal.

3-6-9 Manifestation Techniques

Step 1. Create an affirmation for what you want to manifest. Be clear about what you want.

Step 2. Write the Affirmations.

3 times in the morning.

6 times at noon.

9 times before bedtime.

Visualize your manifestation happening for 30 days.
Stay dedicated - Put in the work by staying focused on your goal.

Time Management and Organization

Having good time management means you are making most of your time by working smarter (recognizing what must be done and doing it the most effective way). Being busy doesn't mean you are effective but being organized and task-oriented means you are focused to thrive.

Recognize the importance of time management. Time Management is about organizing and planning your time appropriately.

One of the main benefits of the organization is a sense of control that allows for increased productivity. For any business, an organization plays a significant role in helping you achieve your goals. Practicing effective organizational skills will help you personally and professionally, and your good organization skills will be reflected in the completion of all your everyday responsibilities.

Benefits of Time Management

Provide a better quality of work – proper utilization of time and prioritization of activities helps you focus on important tasks to work on them with full attention
Productivity & efficiency
Less Procrastination
Less stress and anxiety
Improved quality of life
More opportunities and growth, boost self-esteem
More time for relationships, leisure, and recreation

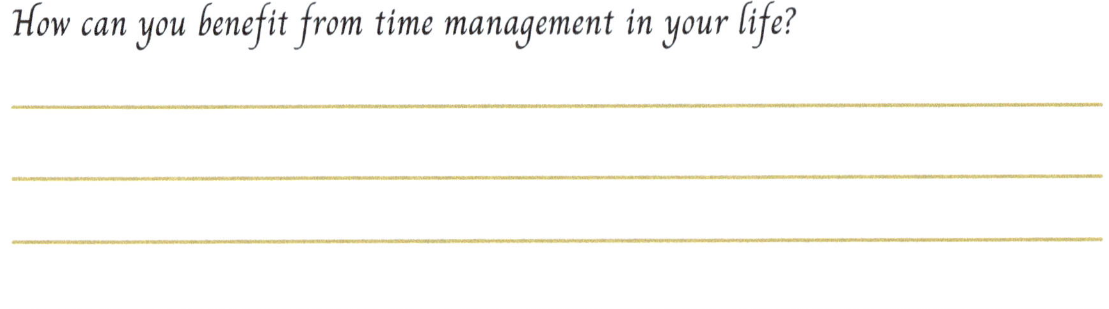
How can you benefit from time management in your life?

When you create your daily plan, stick with it!
Organizing your days and weeks in advance. There will always be surprises, but it's likely that you have an idea of what you need to do daily.
Track your daily and weekly duties to understand what you do and notice patterns

Prioritize
You must figure out which tasks or activities will deliver the best returns. That way, you can prioritize these over less important tasks.

To-Do List
Tasks that maximize your time and energy based on the values and goals that matter the most

Avoid Distractions
According to Gloria Mark, a University of California, Irvine, a professor who studies interruptions, "it takes an average of 23 minutes and 15 seconds to get back to the task."
Try not to multitask or keep it at a minimum- Science has repeatedly shown that trying to do multiple things at once hurts productivity, and it turns out it harms our ability to focus too. A 2009 Stanford study found that heavy media multitaskers struggled to filter out distractions during tests of their cognitive capability.

Put your phone on silent & out of sight- this helps you not to look at your phone keeping your attention on task.

Be Realistic & Flexible
Are you creating an effective to do list? The next page will help you create them.

5 steps to create an effective to do list method:

Before leaving, at the end of your workday, write down the six most important things you need to accomplish tomorrow. Write only six.

____

____

____

____

____

____

Order the six tasks by importance from 1 to 6.

1. ______________________________
2. ______________________________
3. ______________________________
4. ______________________________
5. ______________________________
6. ______________________________

When you arrive in the morning, start by doing your first task. Don't move on until you finished the first one. Don't multitask!

5 steps to create an effective to do list method:

Before leaving, at the end of your workday, write down the six most important things you need to accomplish tomorrow. Write only six.

Order the six tasks by importance from 1 to 6.

1.
2.
3.
4.
5.
6.

When you arrive in the morning, start by doing your first task. Don't move on until you finished the first one. Don't multitask!

5 steps to create an effective to do list method:

Before leaving, at the end of your workday, write down the six most important things you need to accomplish tomorrow. Write only six.

Order the six tasks by importance from 1 to 6.

1.
2.
3.
4.
5.
6.

When you arrive in the morning, start by doing your first task. Don't move on until you finished the first one. Don't multitask!

Process Timeline

When you feel overwhelmed try to break them down to 6 steps.

Step 1:

Step 2:

Step 3:

Step 4:

Step 5:

Step 6:

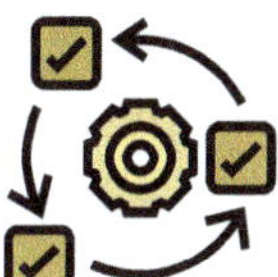

Process Timeline

When you feel overwhelmed try to break them down to 6 steps.

Step 1:

Step 2:

Step 3:

Step 4:

Step 5:

Step 6:

"The feeling of overwhelm is a feeling that will pass when I breathe"

Entrepreneurs and Money Management

Financial literacy is important when owning a business. If someone is struggling with psychological distress, it impacts how they handle their finances. When we are not able to evaluate our past traumas, we struggle to either consciously or subconsciously resolve issues, such as our financial mistakes. Financial trauma negatively impacts our reaction to chronic financial stress on our well-being.

When you are starting your own business, a lot of financial stress can arise, because funds are needed to build your company.
Looking back at your financial history, when was the first time you had credit concerns?

Tips to Take Control of Your Finances & Mental Health

Create a Budget: Know your income and restrict your spending by paying more attention, or by using a budgeting tool.

Talk with a Financial Advisor: A financial advisor gives you access to expert advice on how to deal with money problems. They can help you manage your budget and help with a plan to become financially healthy now and in the future.
Be mindful on your spending: Use a cash or debit card when possible, to eliminate debt build-up.

Educate Yourself About Business Finances: Learn about business credit, funding, grants and other financial resources that will help you thrive in your business. Personal finances are different from business, and you should understand the difference, as education is key to success and will help decrease your financial concerns.

Know That Past Financial Issues Can Affect Your Mental Health:
Life changes such as losing business, mental or physical health problems or relationship issues can be difficult. Debt can make you feel anxious, keeping track of your money may be difficult to do when you are depressed with low energy, and some mental health issues can make money decisions difficult.

Debt Tracker

Debt :

Balance :

Adv. Payment :

DATE	PAYMENT	BALANCE

Debt :

Balance :

Adv. Payment :

DATE	PAYMENT	BALANCE

Debt :

Balance :

Adv. Payment :

DATE	PAYMENT	BALANCE

Debt :

Balance :

Adv. Payment :

DATE	PAYMENT	BALANCE

Monthly Budget

GOAL		
INCOME -1		
INCOME -2		
OTHER INCOME		
	TOTAL INCOME	

EXPENSES
MONTH
BUDGET

BILL TO BE PAID	DUE DATE	AMOUNT	PAID

MONTHLY SUMMARY

TOTAL INCOME	TOTAL EXPENSES	DIFFERENCE

NOTES

Savings Overview

Savings Goals

Actual Savings

What motivates me to save money?

How can I stay motivated to save money?

“I invest money wisely.”

Gratitude/Giving

Gratitude helps foster a positive mindset, and also comes with its own set of health benefits. It improves psychological health, increases mental strength, reduces aggression, and enhances empathy. Gratitude is the feeling of being grateful or thankful. People who are grateful, and show it often, tend to be more optimistic and live happier lives.

Research shows that gratitude is part of the psychological foundation that prompts us to "give back" in many ways. It encourages us to return favors to our community, customers and family members.

Acknowledge where you are in your entrepreneurial journey, be grateful for what you have already accomplished, and show appreciation for your customers, social media following, employees and partners.

Entrepreneurs should have a giving attitude if they want others to invest in their business. This means that entrepreneurs should be willing to help in their community and support other entrepreneurs. Giving is a big part of gratitude because it is a genuine way to be thankful for what you have, and acknowledge that your support helps others. There are other benefits to giving as an entrepreneur. Life has a strong tendency to reflect on us; this is why our energy and actions are so important.

We can make a choice to strive to give more of ourselves. It also means being generous by saying kind words, smiling, investing our time in people, and serving a greater good. Do well by people even when it's not reciprocated.

When we give to others it also models behaviors for people who admire your success and your business self-esteem.

DATE:

I am stepping into the most successful time of my life.

Life Coach VS Psychotherapist

It is important that people are informed and aware of their self-care options when addressing their emotional and mental health. Mental health is very serious because if we do not take care of our mental care needs it leads to mental illness. There is a lot of information that can be misleading to people who are trying to find appropriate resources to receive help. This guide is intended to inform and may not answer all questions about the differences between coaching and therapy but can help you identify questions that you want to ask the professional who is identifying as a coach or therapist.

What is therapy?

It is important that people are informed and aware of their self-care options when addressing their emotional and mental health. Mental health is very serious because if we do not take care of our mental care needs it leads to mental illness. There is a lot of information that can be misleading to people who are trying to find appropriate resources to receive help. This guide is intended to inform and may not answer all questions about the differences between coaching and therapy but can help you identify questions that you want to ask the professional who is identifying as a coach or therapist.

Therapy, also called counseling or psychotherapy, is a long-term process in which a client works with a healthcare professional to diagnose and resolve problematic beliefs, behaviors, relationship issues, feelings, and sometimes, physical responses. The idea behind therapy is to focus on past traumas and issues to change self-destructive habits, repair and improve relationships, and work through painful feelings. Many therapists are branching out into coaching services, and many coaches advertise services that sound a lot like therapy.

Therapists assess, diagnose, and treat mental illness. As such, therapists often focus their work on identifying and reducing symptoms. There are other medical professionals in the field of mental health who are doctors, psychologist and psychiatrist. Psychiatrist diagnose and prescribe psychotropic medication. Sometimes psychotropic medication is needed to help elevate symptoms.

The goal of therapy is to get you to be happier, more settled, and at peace by releasing or unblocking. Therapy, at its core, is working on the psychological problems from the source and doing healing work. You deeply examine the questions and solve them, so that you're able to feel free to move forward.

What is life coaching?

Life coaching is when a client works with a coach who is not a healthcare professional to clarify goals and identify obstacles and problematic behaviors, to create action plans to achieve desired results. A life coach takes the client's current starting point as an acceptable neutral ground, and is action-based from that point forward. With a life coach, you might work on discovering your passions, strategizing a path to achieving them, and building the positive mindset that will empower you to achieve them.

Coaches motivate and encourage people to achieve specific goals. Because it does not involve identifying and reducing symptoms, coaches often describe their work as being more positive in nature.

There is an overlap between therapists and coaches. The overlap includes accomplishing goals and skills. Keep in mind that therapists also offer coaching programs to attract new clients or to add additional maintenance resources to their treatment.

The major difference between therapy and coaching is that coaching is solely focused on setting and achieving goals in their niche (life, financial, holistic health, sex, etc.).

Regulation

States heavily regulate therapy. Typically, therapists must be licensed or working under supervision, and licensure requires a graduate degree, along with significant additional experience. Consumers can file a complaint with the therapist's state licensing board when they feel their therapist is working unprofessionally.

Coaching, on the other hand, is largely unregulated. Anyone can call himself or herself a "coach" and open a coaching business, regardless of training or experience. Coaching is a legitimate field with growing research and a code of ethics, but adherence to that code of ethics is voluntary. There are coaches who have life experiences and others who have education in their chosen niche.

Informed Decision

Hopefully, this information will guide you in deciding what would be the most appropriate treatment for you. This information is intended to be informative, and a full decision on the profession that you choose should be made with a professional. It is important that you learn what options you have when making an informed decision. Also, be aware that you can opt to use a therapist and a coach at the same time, as long as they're informed that you've employed both their services, and they've signed a release of information form, so they can collaborate on goals and treatment planning.

Comparison Chart

	Psychotherapist	Coach
TraumaInformed	x	x*
Mental Health Symptoms that cause distress	x	
Trauma Treatment	x	*
Navigating emotions & mood	x	
Accomplishing Goals	x	x
Accelerating to Next Steps	x	x
Improve Relationship skills that include intimacy & pleasure	x	x ★
Stop unhelpful habits and replace with healthy ones.	x	x
Negative thoughts or Inner Critic	x	x
Struggle with interpersonal relationships and want to learn strategies to feel less impacted by others.	x	

**Coaches can also have education to specialize in certain areas, but you should ask questions about their experience and understand what it means. Being trauma informed and doing trauma treatment is different. Coaches who focus on mental health should be aware of their scope of practice for legal reasons.*

Questions to Ask a Coach or Therapist

What is your goal with working with me?
Do you specialize in anything particularly?
Do you have a certification or license?
How would you know if I need additional resources?
How long have you been practicing?
How much do you charge?
Describe your ideal client?
What is a typical session like?
How long are sessions?

Think of any other questions that you would like to ask.

DATE:

I am now creating my life exactly how I want it.

DATE:

Sometimes, I will have bad days and that is ok.

DATE:

The feeling of overwhelm is a feeling that will pass when I breathe.

DATE:

I can achieve any goal that I set for myself.

DATE:

My income is consistently increasing.

DATE:

I am confident in my brand and mission.

DATE:

I am proud of myself and all I have accomplished.

DATE:

Negative thoughts have no power over me.

DATE:

I choose not to criticize myself or others.

DATE:

I am the definition of prosperity.

DATE:

I am not my mistakes.

DATE:

I choose faith over fear.

DATE:

I have the power to create change.

DATE:

I believe in me.

DATE:

I am worthy of acceptance.

DATE:

I invest money wisely.

DATE:

I choose to let go of everyone and everything that no longer serve me.
I am a gracious giver and receiver.

DATE:

I will take time to heal.

DATE:

I will take time to rest.

DATE:

I am free of worry.

DATE:

I am debt-free.

DATE:

I generate wealth.

DATE:

I am going to take the next step.

DATE:

I have everything I need in me.

DATE:

I get to create my own definition of success.

DATE:

I am allowed to say no.

DATE:

My business path is unique to me.

DATE:

My time is valuable.

DATE:

I can have a successful career and successful relationships.

DATE:

My actions create constant prosperity.

DATE:

Today will be another successful day.

DATE:

I can be both a work in progress and an impactful leader.

DATE:

I have the knowledge and skills required to create the business of my dreams.

DATE:

My talents are worthy of being paid for abundantly.

DATE:

Success and prosperity effortlessly flow to me.

DATE:

I am thankful for my creativity and my skills for getting me this far.

DATE:

I am thankful for everyone who has contributed to my business success.

DATE:

I am grateful for all that I have and all that I will accomplish.

DATE:

I am dependable and resourceful.

DATE:

I am a positive person who attracts positive situations for success.

DATE:

I am worthy of the success coming my way.

DATE:

My journey is my journey, and I will not compare my journey to others.

DATE:

My past mistakes do not define me, but they have helped me grow.

DATE:

I will ask for help and support when needed.

DATE:

My work makes a difference.

DATE:

My business is a huge success.

DATE:

I believe in myself and trust in my abilities to succeed in all that I do.

DATE:

Being successful is natural for me.

DATE:

I attract my ideal clients and customers with my energy.

DATE:

I create wonderful business opportunities every day.

DATE:

I love the freedom my business produces for me.

DATE:

Being my own boss is a responsibility I handle with care.

DATE:

People love what I do; they love my products and my services.

DATE:

I make good decisions.

Conclusion

In our business we visualize success. However, we don't talk about the emotional/mental struggles with striving for success. Owning a business is a great accomplishment but thriving in a business takes different kinds of skills. Hopefully, this journal has been able to guide you to self-reflect and identify ways in taking care of your emotional needs, improve your self-esteem, and to excel your business self-esteem.

Here is a list of directory websites that can help you find a therapist if you notice you may need one to address mental health, trauma, mental illness, or self-esteem.

https://www.cliniciansofcolor.org/
https://latinxtherapy.com/
https://samhin.org/provider-directory
https://therapyforblackgirls.com/
Www.therapyforblackmen.org
Www.psychologytoday.com
Www.melaninandmentalhealth.com
Www.nqttcn.com
Www.betterhelp.com
Www.networktherapy.com
Www.therapyforLatinx.com

www.ingramcontent.com/pod-product-compliance
Lightning Source LLC
Chambersburg PA
CBHW082058090726
47909CB00011B/3079

* 9 7 8 0 5 7 8 3 6 2 4 7 2 *